A Day at the Apple Orchard

Text by Megan Faulkner

Photographs by Adam Krawesky

Scholastic Canada Ltd.

Toronto New York London Auckland Sydney
Mexico City New Delhi Hong Kong Buenos Aires

For my wonderful Mum and Dad, and for
Maddie and Max — the apples of my eye.
M.F.

Acknowledgements: Special thanks to Flora-Jane Hartford and her students at the Halton Waldorf School: Allison, Ashanté, Catiyana, Helene, Jackson and Jorren, for their enthusiasm and great smiles! Also to their families, especially Sydney, Maralyn and Colleen, for their help and patience. Thanks to Sara Fayle for allowing us to feed her children copious amounts of chocolate before dinner. For our springtime shots, we'd like to thank Puddicombe Farms for granting us access to their orchard. We'd also like to acknowledge and thank the people at Chudleigh's for all of their kind assistance and allowing us access to their amazing apple orchard. Also, thanks to Jane and Dave for being such great guides! The author wishes to thank George W. Bassel, Ph.D. Candidate, Dept. of Botany, University of Guelph, for his enthusiastic counsel.

p.3 Apple after summer rain © A.G.E. Foto Stock/Firstlight
p.4 Apple orchard covered with snow © Index Stock/Fotosearch
p.5 Frosted bud © Soda/Scholastic Inc.
p.8 Blooming apple orchard © Photodisc/Fotosearch
p.9 Apple ovaries © Soda/Scholastic Inc.
p.17 © Photographer Paul S. Wells WildernessShare.com
p.27 © John McIntosh: Courtesy of the Ontario Agricultural Hall of Fame Association located at Country Heritage Park, Milton, Ontario, Canada.
p.26, 30 "Chas" © Jennifer MacKinnon and Paul Hoffmann

Library and Archives Canada Cataloguing in Publication
Faulkner, Megan
A day at the apple orchard / Megan Faulkner ; photographs by Adam Krawesky.
ISBN 0-439-95713-3
1. Apples--Juvenile literature. 2. Orchards--Juvenile literature.
I. Krawesky, Adam II. Title.
SB363.F39 2005   j634'.11   C2004-905801-0

6 5 4 3 2 1   Printed in Canada   05 06 07 08 09

It's a sunny day in early fall — perfect for apple picking!

Before we go into the orchard, we learn how apples are grown.

It has taken many
months for them to
grow and ripen.

Just like all living things,
apples need the right
amount of rain and sun
to be healthy.

The life of an apple begins in spring. During the winter months, the tree doesn't grow or change. This stage is called dormancy.

Warm weather awakens the tree and it begins a new cycle of growth.

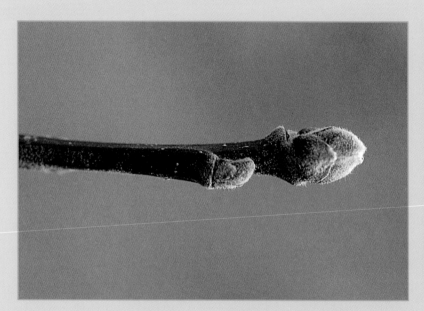

Leaves push out from the tiny buds.

Five-petal blossoms grow in beautiful shades of pink or white.

Apple farmers set up beehives in the orchard.

When a honeybee lands on an apple blossom, it sips the sweet nectar. Tiny grains of pollen stick to its legs.

As the bee flies from flower to flower, the pollen it carries fertilizes the blossoms.

This is called pollination.

As spring turns into summer, the flower petals fall from the trees.

On the branches, ovaries begin to grow. They will become apples.

All summer long the apples get bigger and bigger.

As autumn approaches, the apples start to ripen. They turn from green to red.

Some types of apple, like Granny Smith, stay green. Others, such as Golden Delicious, turn yellow.

By late summer or early fall, the apples are fully ripened.

It's harvest time!

We pick up our baskets and get ready for a tractor ride.

The tractor takes us into the orchard.
We're picking Empire apples today
because they are the ripest.

Before we start, we learn the best way to pick an apple.

Instead of pulling it off the tree, we must turn the "eye" (the bottom) to the sky and tug gently. We want to make sure that the bud is not damaged for next year.

It's time to start picking!

15

Apples bruise easily, so we place them very gently into the basket.

While we are picking, we see wire guards at the bottom of the trees. We aren't the only ones who like apple trees!

Apple farmers must safeguard the trees from hungry creatures such as rabbits, rodents and insects.

Our baskets are full! It's time to head back to the farm!

Now we sample the apples. Crisp and delicious!

Next we see how apple juice and cider are made with an old-fashioned hand press.

First the apples are put in the press.

Then we turn the crank.

The cider comes out the bottom.

Then we have a taste test!

It's been so much fun learning about apples.

We can't wait to come back next year!

Amazing Apple Facts

- Canadians eat an average of 86 apples per year.

- The apple is a member of the rose family.

- It's better not to peel an apple because that's the part with the most vitamins.

- Apples bruise more easily than eggshells break.

- The science of apple growing is called Pomology.

- Apples that grow in the wild are called crab apples. They are usually very sour and not good to eat.

- Apples are Canada's most important tree crop.

There are over 7000 varieties of apples in the world. But only about 100 of these varieties are grown in North America. McIntosh, Red Delicious, Spartan, Empire, Ida Red and Cortland are just some of the apples that we grow in Canada.

Apple Bits

Why do apples turn brown when you bite them?

When you break the skin of an apple, air gets inside. The oxygen in the air reacts with the cells inside the apple and causes them to turn brown. This process is called oxidation. Dipping a freshly cut apple slice in lemon juice will stop it from turning brown, because the vitamin C in the juice acts as an antioxidant.

Did you know that apples have gas?

Apples produce a gas called ethylene that causes them to ripen. If you store apples in a plastic bag, the gas cannot escape and the apples ripen faster.

Bigger isn't always better . . .

Apple farmers prefer to use dwarf trees rather than standard apple trees. The smaller the tree, the easier it is to reach  the apples without a ladder. Shorter trees are easier to prune, and farmers can fit more trees on their land.

Apples in Canada

Apples arrived in Canada about 400 years ago. French settlers brought them to Nova Scotia. By 1850 apple trees could also be found in Quebec, Ontario, the Prairies and British Columbia.

Portrait of John McIntosh

Canada's most famous apple is the McIntosh apple. It was discovered in 1796 by John McIntosh in Dundas County, Ontario. While clearing land on his new farm, McIntosh found several apple trees and transplanted them to the family orchard. By 1811, the sweet, crisp red apples from one of the trees had become popular with friends and neighbours. They called them "granny apples." In 1835, a farmhand working on the McIntosh farm taught John's son, Allen, how to propagate the tree so that even more McIntosh apples could grow.

From then on, the McIntosh family specialized in growing and selling their unique apple. Now the McIntosh is grown in orchards across Canada and the United States. It is also shipped around the world. Every single McIntosh apple tree is a descendant of the first tree from Dundas County.

Chocolate Covered Apples

Here's a yummy apple treat that you can make at home.
You may want to ask an adult to help you.

- 6 cold, medium-size apples
- 6 Popsicle sticks
- 500 g of semi-sweet chocolate, cut into chunks
- 250 ml of any of the following toppings:
  toffee pieces, chocolate chips, candy, nuts or
  anything else you'd like!

3. Put the chunks of chocolate in a bowl and slowly melt them in the microwave. Set it on medium power for about two minutes. Make sure you stir halfway through the heating time. You want the chocolate to be warm and smooth, but not hot.

1. Twist off the apple stems.

2. Push a Popsicle stick down into the core. Make sure you don't push it all the way through.

4. Dip each apple into the chocolate. Make sure you dunk it far enough to cover the whole apple. It's okay if some of the chocolate drips back into the bowl.

5. Put your topping on a plate. Using your fingers or a spoon, sprinkle the topping over the apple as you turn it. You can use the Popsicle stick to turn the apple and make sure it's covered.

6. Set the dipped apples on a cookie sheet lined with wax paper.

7. Refrigerate until the chocolate is set.

8. Enjoy!

NOTES:

Page 3 – The Role of Sunlight

Farmers prune their apple trees so that sunlight can reach the fruit. The sun helps the apple make sugar. In some varieties, like McIntosh, the sun can make the apple redder and sweeter. Because only half the fruit usually faces the sun, that side will turn red while the rest stays green. The red side of the fruit actually has more sugar, so if you share a McIntosh with someone, you may want to share both colours.

Page 7 – Pollination

When the bees are in the orchard, they fly from flower to flower, collecting grains of pollen on their legs. Every time they land on a new flower, the pollen on their legs brushes against the pistil in the centre of the blossom. This fertilizes the blossom so that fruit can grow. Apple blossoms need to be fertilized with pollen from a different type of apple tree to make fruit.

Page 17 – Enemies

Keeping apple trees healthy and safe from enemies is a year-round job. In the winter, rodents sometimes burrow under the snow to nibble on the trees. Farmers put metal guards around the bottom of the trees to protect them. If they didn't do this, the rodents might nibble too much of the bark and cut the roots off from the rest of the tree. With no way of moving nutrients from the roots to the branches, the trees would die.

Farmers check the trees for diseases like Apple Scab, Powdery Mildew, Fire Blight and Cedar Apple Rust. Insects can also be dangerous for apple trees. Worms, caterpillars, aphids and many other hungry creatures can ruin an orchard if they are not stopped. Not all insects are harmful, however: ladybugs, beetles, lacewings and hover flies help farmers by feeding on the insects that eat the trees. And of course we already know how helpful honeybees are!